D1540529

DECADES OF THE 20th AND 21st CENTURIES

The 1920s

Stephen Feinstein

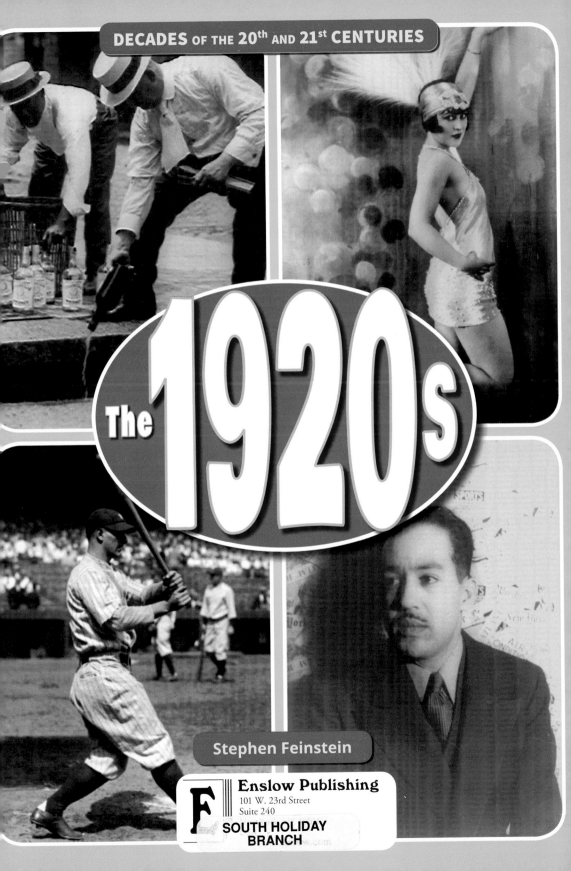

DECADES OF THE 20th AND 21st CENTURIES

The 1920s

Stephen Feinstein

Enslow Publishing
101 W. 23rd Street
Suite 240

Published in 2016 by Enslow Publishing, LLC.
101 W. 23rd Street, Suite 240, New York, NY 10011

Library of Congress Cataloging-in-Publication Data
Feinstein, Stephen.
The 1920s / Stephen Feinstein.
      pages cm. — (Decades of the 20th and 21st centuries)
Includes bibliographical references and index.
Summary: "Discusses the decade 1920-1929 in the United States in terms of culture, art, science, and politics"—Provided by publisher.
Audience: Grade 9 to 12.
ISBN 978-0-7660-6924-4
1. United States—Civilization—1918-1945—Juvenile literature. 2. United States—Politics and government—1923-1929—Juvenile literature. 3. United States—Politics and govern-ment—1921-1923—Juvenile literature. 4. Nineteen twenties—Juvenile literature. I. Title.
E169.1.F3545 2015
973.91'4—dc23
                                    2015010944

Printed in the United States of America

To Our Readers: We have done our best to make sure all Web sites in this book were active and appropriate when we went to press. However, the author and the publisher have no control over and assume no liability for the material available on those Web sites or on any Web sites they may link to. Any comments or suggestions can be sent by e-mail to customerservice@enslow.com.

Photo Credits: Albert Harlingue/Roger Viollet/Getty Images, pp. 64, 89 (top); Ann Ronan Pictures/Print Collector/Getty Images, pp. 75, 87 (top); Apic/Getty Images, p. 79; Bennett/Getty Images, p. 43; Eddie Jackson/NY Daily News Archive via Getty Images, p. 59; English Heritage/Heritage Images/Getty Images, pp. 24, 42, 50; FPG/Archive Photos/Getty Images, p. 73; Hulton Archive/Getty Image, pp. 26, 31, 49, 71, 76, 85 (top and bottom); Keystone-France/Gamma-Key-stone via Getty Images, pp. 13, 68, 80, 88 (bottom); Keystone/Getty Images, p. 39; Kidwiler Col-lection/Diamond Images/Getty Images, pp. 3 (bottom left), 40; Library of Congress/Moviepix/Getty Images, pp. 3 (top right), 21; Library of Congress Prints & Photographs Division, National Photo Company Collection, p. 3 (top left); Library of Congress, Prints & Photographs Division, Carl Van Vechten Collection, p. 3 (bottom right); Margaret Bourke-White/The LIFE Images Collection/Getty Images, p. 17; MPI/Getty Images, pp. 6, 55, 56; New York Times Co./Getty Im-ages, p. 45, 87 (bottom); Photo12/UIG via Getty Images, pp. 53, 60; PhotoQuest/Getty Images, pp. 47, 88 (top); Sasha/Getty Images, p. 22; stockelements/Shutterstock.com, p. 37; Underwood Archives/Getty Images, pp. 10, 14, 18, 29, 86 (top), 89 (bottom); Universal History Archive/UIG via Getty Images, pp. 63, 86 (bottom); Transcendental Graphics/Getty Images, pp. 35, 67.

Cover Credits: Kidwiler Collection/Diamond Images/Getty Images (Lou Gehrig); Library of Congress, Prints & Photographs Division, Carl Van Vechten Collection (Langston Hughes); Library of Congress/Moviepix/Getty Images (flapper); Library of Congress Prints & Photographs Division, National Photo Company Collection (pouring whiskey down a drain).

Contents

The 1920s were known as the Roaring Twenties.

Introduction

For many Americans, the 1920s—often referred to as the Roaring Twenties—were a period of prosperity with rapid growth in industry and new developments in the arts and entertainment. But the decade did not begin on an optimistic note. Although America and its allies had won World War I in 1918, the end of the war led to an economic slump. A deadly flu that claimed more than twenty million victims around the world spread in 1918 and 1919. The weary survivors wished to celebrate.

The American economy began to recover and eventually prosper during the Republican administrations of Presidents Warren G. Harding and Calvin Coolidge. Both presidents encouraged the growth of big business. When Calvin Coolidge said, "the business of America is business," the nation took his words to heart.

Factories that had once made weapons and supplies for the war now made peacetime products, such as washing machines, vacuum cleaners, radios, and other household items. If people didn't have enough money to buy these new products, they borrowed from banks—often more than they could afford to repay. Unpaid debt would become a serious problem by the middle of the decade.

Americans worked hard, but they also played hard. Not deterred by Prohibition—the ban on alcoholic beverages—many Americans went to speakeasies. There, thanks to gangsters, such as Chicago's Al Capone, who smuggled and sold illegal liquor, people could swig alcoholic drinks while dancing the Charleston to jazz, music pioneered by African-American musicians a few years earlier in New Orleans. The birth of broadcast radio in 1920 spurred jazz's popularity. The Harlem

Renaissance promoted a flourishing of African-American literature and arts in the neighborhood of Harlem in New York during the 1920s.

Women called flappers wore skirts with scandalously short hemlines. Having just won the right to vote, women felt freer to express themselves in new ways.

The rich became richer during the decade, but many poor people did not benefit at all from the country's economic growth. Many Americans became fearful of newcomers to the nation's shores. Laws were passed to limit the number of immigrants allowed into the country each year. Only a small number of people from eastern and southern Europe were allowed, and Asians were kept out entirely. The public also lost faith in its leaders. Corrupt politicians took bribes. The government was rocked by scandals. Finally, the 1920s saw the return of a hate group called the Ku Klux Klan.

Three world leaders—a dictator in Italy, a brutal leader in Germany, and a new emperor in Japan—first entered the spotlight during the 1920s and would later help start World War II.

Meanwhile, many Americans invested in the stock market. But the stock market could not climb forever. A frenzy of speculation and carefree spending ended in the great stock market crash of 1929. The party was over.

Pop Culture, Lifestyles, and Fashion

The 1920s is one of the most fascinating periods in modern history. This decade, known as the Roaring Twenties, still captures our imaginations today. During the 1920s, the standard of living rose for most Americans, including the working poor even though the majority of Americans worked long hours for very low wages. Basic utilities, such as natural gas, running water, and electricity became increasingly available in the home. Local governments provided water and sewage treatment and garbage collection. People lived healthier lives. With hot and cold running water, people bathed more frequently. By 1929, 71 percent of American homes had indoor bathrooms. With electric lights in the home, there was less danger of fire from kerosene lamps and gaslights. And thanks to gas stoves, the air inside the home was now free of coal dust and kerosene fumes. Middle- and upper-class families could afford to buy new electric appliances, such as vacuum cleaners, washing machines, and refrigerators.

Radio broadcasts became a source for news and entertainment.

Telephones and Radios

New forms of communication brought Americans closer to each other. The telephone, and then the radio, brought about major changes in the way Americans lived and worked. In 1915, coast-to-coast telephone service had begun. By 1921, 13 percent of Americans had telephones. A person on the West Coast was only a phone call away from someone on the East Coast. At the beginning of the decade, most Americans still wrote letters to stay in touch with distant relatives or friends. But as the years went by, more people had telephones in their homes. The telephone became essential in the business world.

On November 2, 1920, even as most Americans had yet to have a telephone conversation, another amazing device was introduced to the nation. On that day, the radio station KDKA in Pittsburgh, Pennsylvania, broadcast the nation's first scheduled public radio program. Only a small number of Americans got to hear the news broadcast that day on their brand new radio sets. But practically overnight, excitement about this new form of communication spread. By 1923, more than five hundred radio stations were broadcasting. Radio sales that year reached $60 million.

Listening to favorite radio shows became a popular family activity. As more Americans bought radios and tuned into broadcasts that featured music, sports, or news, American businesses began advertising on the radio. During the second half of the decade, hundreds of radio stations were linked to form the two major radio networks, NBC and CBS. By the end of the decade, radios could be found in more than half the homes in America, and sales of radios had grown to more than $842 million a year. In a single decade, radio had become a huge business and a major part of Americans' lives.

Automobiles

Freedom is such a basic part of American culture that it was not at all surprising when Americans fell in love with the machine that gave them the ability to go wherever they wanted whenever they wanted. Americans began buying cars as soon as they became available. In the 1920s, Henry Ford's Model T became the most popular automobile. Ford had lowered the price so even the workers in his plants could afford to buy one. New Model Ts could be purchased for a few hundred dollars. A used Model T in good condition could be bought for as little as fifty dollars. There was such a high demand for the Model T that in 1925 Ford's assembly lines claimed they completed a new Model T every ten seconds.

In 1927, Ford was facing increasing competition from General Motors' Chevrolet. To keep up, Ford introduced his Model A. The Model A was generally considered a vast improvement over the Model T. It quickly became the most popular car in America.

By 1927, the automobile had changed the lifestyle of millions of Americans. Many middle- and upper-class Americans moved to new suburbs because the car gave them a convenient way to commute to jobs in the city. By 1929, there were more than twenty-three million cars on America's roads.

Planes and Trains

Passenger transportation took a great leap forward during the 1920s. Americans who needed to get from one city to another or from coast to coast could travel in luxury aboard plush trains. Throughout the decade, railroads were the preferred means of transportation. However, in 1927, another travel option became available. On May 20, Charles Lindbergh made the first successful solo transatlantic flight from New York to Paris aboard his little plane, the *Spirit of St. Louis*. The nonstop flight covered 3,610 miles and took 33 hours and

Lucky Lindy

Charles Lindbergh had never been afraid of airplanes. At age twenty, he dropped out of college to attend flying school. Afterward, he worked as a stunt pilot. He also delivered airmail. Then Lindbergh began planning a nonstop flight from New York to Paris. There was a $25,000 prize for the first pilot to succeed. Many had tried before and failed. Some pilots had even died during the attempts. Regardless, Lindbergh was confident. His plane was the single-engine *Spirit of St. Louis*. He took off from New York on the morning of May 20, 1927. He touched down in Paris more than thirty-three hours later. The entire world celebrated this new hero. Lindbergh returned home to parades and medals. Many people instantly lost their fear of flying. Suddenly, everybody wanted to be like Lucky Lindy.

Barrels of beer were destroyed during Prohibition.

29 minutes. Lucky Lindy had made aviation history. He became an instant hero.

Less then three months after Lindbergh's epic flight, no fewer than eight airlines were offering regularly scheduled flights between various American cities. Earlier in the decade, airplanes had been used to deliver the mail. Now, airlines hoped to attract passengers, too. Although business was slow at first, the airlines could rightfully claim that they would get you there faster, although the trip would cost more. For example, in 1927, a trip from New York to Boston took five and a half hours by train and cost eight dollars. It took only three hours by plane but cost thirty dollars. And one could travel from Chicago to San Francisco in sixty-eight hours by train at a cost of eighty dollars, while it would take only twenty-two and a half hours by plane but at a cost of two hundred dollars.

Prohibition

In 1920, the US government outlawed alcohol. The Eighteenth Amendment to the Constitution banned the manufacture, transportation, and sale of intoxicating liquors. The move toward Prohibition began as early as the 1830s. Rowdy saloons existed in nearly every American town and city. These unruly bars often played host to gambling and drunken violence. Some states adopted anti-saloon laws. Dry organizations, such as the Women's Christian Temperance Union and the Anti-Saloon League, eventually succeeded in winning enough support to ensure passage of the amendment. Congress proposed a nationwide liquor ban. The states ratified it in January 1919, and alcohol was officially prohibited in the United States as of January 16, 1920.

As America entered the era of Prohibition, the new law seemed certain to put the thousands of bars around the country out of business. But it would take more than a new law on the books to change the lifestyles of millions of Americans. The bars did indeed close down, but many of them soon reopened as speakeasies. Hidden away in rooms beneath or in the back of the former bars, the speakeasies served alcoholic drinks to customers who typically gained entry by giving secret passwords, often something such as "Joe sent me." The term speakeasy referred to the password ritual. Some speakeasies were simple bars where people sat, drank, and talked. Others were elegant nightclubs where, in addition to drinking, customers were entertained by elaborate floor shows and danced to the music of lively jazz bands.

Considering that the main business of the speakeasies was against the law, how did they stay in business? After all, their locations were certainly known to the police. There is a simple answer to this question—bribery. Owners of speakeasies made regular payments to the police. Also bribing the police were gangsters known as bootleggers—powerful mob bosses, such as Al Capone and Bugs Moran—who sold the illegal liquor to the club owners. Of course, not all law officials were corrupt. Some businesses did close, if only temporarily, when the management and their customers were hauled off by the police after a surprise raid. But in general, Prohibition seemed to have created a win-win situation for the speakeasy owners, their customers, gangsters, and the police.

The situation caused a massive increase in corruption and the growth of organized crime. Powerful gangsters murdered anybody who got in their way. Machine guns and bulletproof getaway cars became essential elements of the gangster lifestyle. To many Americans, gangsters seemed to be heroic figures because of their defiance of authority. And the people who went to speakeasies believed that bootleggers were performing a useful service to society. But as gang violence grew worse, the romance faded. The final straw came on St. Valentine's Day in 1929, when seven men were massacred

Patrons could find alcohol at hidden bars called speakeasies.

Al Capone

America's best-known gangster was Al Capone. He ruled Chicago for most of the decade. Capone began his criminal career in New York. At the age of twenty, he moved to Chicago, where he quickly amassed wealth and power as owner of a network of speakeasies and casinos. Capone's public image of a generous and kindhearted man gained him the respect and admiration of many city residents. However, he was ruthless with his rivals. Capone's men executed seven members of a rival gang in cold blood in the St. Valentine's Day Massacre. After this slaughter, the federal government began investigating him. He was charged with income tax evasion and sentenced to eleven years in prison. Despite Capone's imprisonment, gangsters continued to flourish. Prohibition had the unexpected effect of helping organized crime take root in America. It would thrive for the rest of the Prohibition era and well beyond.

in a gangland killing ordered by Al Capone. Ultimately, Prohibition proved to have been a mistake. It would be repealed in 1933.

Feminists

Many American women in the 1920s, especially of the younger generation, were eager to challenge society's traditional notions about the proper role for women. The women's suffrage movement, which had officially begun at the Seneca Falls Women's Rights Convention in 1848, ended with the ratification of the Nineteenth Amendment to the Constitution on August 18, 1920.

Having won the right to vote, feminists now sought to bring about equality of the sexes. The League of Women Voters sought greater educational opportunities for women and fought to eliminate laws that discriminated against women. The Women's Trade Union League (WTUL) fought to improve working conditions for women. And in 1921, Margaret Sanger founded the American Birth Control League, which would change its name to the Planned Parenthood Federation of America in 1942. The organization provided women with information about birth control.

Other feminists favored a more radical approach to women's rights. Alice Paul, the leader of the National Women's Party, led the fight for the passage of an Equal Rights Amendment (ERA) that would guarantee equal rights under the Constitution. Many women, however, considered the ERA too extreme. Many decades later in the 1970s, feminists were still fighting for the ERA, but it was ultimately defeated.

Flappers

While feminists sought to bring about change through political activism, other women brought about change in a different way. Young women who felt that they should be able to enjoy the same social and sexual freedoms as men came to be known as flappers. Such women hung out at speakeasies, danced, smoked cigarettes, drank bootleg liquor, and partied late into the night. More conservative members of society were shocked at the flappers' use of heavy makeup and outrageous dresses that revealed legs in silk stockings. Even worse, flappers kissed men in public and seemed to enjoy flaunting their irreverent behavior.

Flappers set the style for 1920s women who considered themselves free from traditional styles of dress. The typical flapper look was basically tubular—a little-boy look that de-emphasized a woman's naturally curved form. The breasts were flattened, the waist was dropped to the hipline, and skirts kept creeping upward until they ended just below the knee. Flappers wore silk or rayon stockings with garter belts or rolled-over garters above the knee and black patent leather high-heeled shoes.

Because the flapper look required women to be thin, many women became obsessed with watching their weight. Tight corsets were replaced by looser, more comfortable undergarments.

Flappers wore their hair short, which was influenced by movie star Clara Bow. They hardly went anywhere without their bell-shaped, tight-fitting cloche hats—cloche means bell in French. In the evenings, however, flappers would often replace their hats with more exotic items, such as a jeweled comb or an ostrich-plume headdress. Formal evening wear often consisted of floor-length backless evening dresses that were often accompanied by long strings of beads. Other accessories, such as scarves, handbags, jewelry, and cigarette cases, were an important part of the flapper look.

The tubular look was not limited to women in the 1920s. Young men's fashion also began to assume a tubular look. Men wore narrow-shouldered jackets that hung straight to the hips and wide loose-fitting pants. Around 1925, college men adopted Oxford bags,

The outrageous clothing and behavior of flappers shocked traditionalists.

The Origin of Flappers

Nobody is sure where the term *flapper* came from. It may have referred to a young bird boldly flapping its wings while learning to fly. It may also have been based on a popular fashion trend. In the 1920s, a young woman often left her overcoat unbuttoned so that it flapped back and forth as she walked.

a more extreme style of wide-legged pants that originated at Oxford University in England. Oxford bags were so wide that the wearer appeared to be swimming in them. They typically measured about twenty-five inches around the knees and twenty-two inches around the cuffs. Also popular with college men were the raccoon coat and the belted Burberry trench coat, which was another item influenced by British fashion.

Dancing Until They Dropped

Many flappers went wild over a dance called the Charleston. The Charleston supposedly originated with African-American dancers in Charleston, South Carolina. It was characterized by fast-paced, jerky movements—a knock-kneed, heel-kicking, hip-swinging dance. While it tended to display the body because it required the dancers to wear loose clothing, the Charleston had a cheerful, saucy effect rather than being seductive or sexy. People had so much fun dancing and watching the Charleston that a Charleston dance craze soon swept the nation.

Before long, dancers were competing in Charleston contests. In 1924, a Charleston marathon at New York's Roseland Ballroom lasted for twenty-four hours. Such dance marathons took place throughout the decade all around the country. During the 1920s, many Americans seemed determined to dance until they dropped. The main motivation was the cash prize awarded to the winning couple. Young couples would dance for hour after hour—often day after day—struggling to keep moving. Often one or the other dance partner would fall asleep, and the other would have to keep moving while supporting the sleeping partner. One by one, couples would collapse until one last couple staggered or crawled across the floor to collect the prize.

Among the more notable marathon dancers was Alma Cummings, who danced for a record-setting twenty-seven hours in New York in 1923. Her endurance seemed impressive until June Curry danced for ninety hours in Cleveland that same year. Also in 1923, Homer Morehouse danced for eighty-seven hours. Unfortunately, Morehouse literally danced until he dropped—dead!

Crossword Puzzles

In 1924, many Americans were spending their free time poring over clues to come up with the correct words to fill crossword puzzle grids.

Crossword puzzles became a national craze touched off by the publication of Richard Leo Simon and Max Lincoln Schuster's collection of crossword puzzles, *The Crossword Puzzle Book*. After the huge success of their first book, Simon and Schuster went on to build one of America's major publishing companies.

Before long, crossword puzzle contests were being held on college campuses. The University of Kentucky even offered a course in crossword puzzles. People could be seen working on crossword puzzles while dining in cafeterias, enjoying picnics, or traveling on the train. Crossword puzzles must have been especially popular on the Baltimore and Ohio Railroad because the railroad supplied dictionaries to passengers.

Day by Day in Every Way

While millions of Americans in 1924 were searching for the right words to fill in their crossword puzzles, many others believed that they had found a few special words that had the power to transform their lives. These people had come across French psychotherapist Emile Coué's book about the power of mind over matter, *Self-Mastery Through Conscious Auto-Suggestion*. Coué's system was easy—all you had to do was repeat the same twelve-word sentence over and over again. For the next few years, Americans could be heard uttering the words, "Day by day in every way I am getting better and better."

Every decade seems to bring forth con artists who manage to make a lot of money from the wishful thinking of gullible people. In the 1920s, many Americans were convinced that thanks to Emile Coué, the secret to good health and happiness was suddenly within their grasp. After all, Coué pointed to some miraculous cures that he attributed to his system. For example, one man had been cured of excessive yawning. And two boys who stuttered were now able to say without stuttering, "Good morning," and "I won't stutter anymore." Of course,

Even actress Doris Kenyon enjoyed working on crossword puzzles.

Many Americans hoped Emile Coué's affirmations would cure them.

Coué was never able to prove that his system had actually cured any serious problem. After a time, most Americans realized that if something sounds too good to be true, it is, and they swiftly abandoned Coué and his amazing twelve words.

An Ancient Chinese Game Becomes Popular

Millions of Americans in the 1920s suddenly found themselves uttering strange-sounding words, such as Pung and Chow, and discussing Red Dragon, South Wind, and bamboo. They had become devoted fans of Mah-Jongg, an ancient Chinese game that was sweeping the United States. The game had complicated rules that were always changing, and serious players studied rule books to keep up. The game was played with a set of 144 carved bone tiles, which were arranged on green-baize tables at elegant Mah-Jongg parties. Mah-Jongg sets were available in a wide range of prices. A fancy set could cost as much as $500, while a more humble set could be bought for just a few dollars. Many women stopped playing bridge and formed Mah-Jongg clubs instead.

Stunts from On High

It seems that some people will do anything for money. A surprisingly large number of Americans during the 1920s participated in many kinds of wild and crazy stunts. Perhaps it was the general optimism of the times that led such people to believe that any stunt was worth trying. In the early 1920s, veteran pilots performed aerial stunts in rural America. They came to be called barnstormers. Sometimes, they would literally storm barns by swooping down to drop a chunk of ice on the roof. They would then land and bet the farmer that it would hail soon even though the weather was clear and warm. They then took off and landed again, pointed out the ice to the farmer, took the farmer's money, and laughed all the way to the bank.

Other popular aerial stunts involved wing-walking. The stunt person would climb out of his or her seat, usually in a two-seater plane, and walk out on the wing while performing various tricks as the plane's pilot carried out some tricky maneuvers. Although the wing-walker was protected by a leather and steel harness fastened to bracing wires, accidents often happened. Planes crashed, and wing-walkers and barnstormers were often killed. The aerial stunt business was dangerous. One barnstormer and wing-walker of the early 1920s who was not killed was pilot Charles Lindbergh.

Although flagpole sitters did not climb nearly as high into the air as the barnstormers, they remained above the ground for a much longer time. The flagpole-sitting fad began in Hollywood in 1924 when a theater hired Alvin "Shipwreck" Kelly to sit on top of a flagpole fifty feet above the ground to draw crowds. For thirteen hours, Kelly sat on a small rubber-padded seat strapped to the ball of the flagpole. He proved to be such a sensation that he was soon being hired by theaters and hotels all around the country. In 1927 in St. Louis, he sat on a flagpole for a record thirteen days! Flagpole sitting soon became a fad, and other people began sitting on flagpoles. In 1929, Kelly spent 145 days on flagpoles. That year in Baltimore, twenty people sat atop flagpoles during one week. Three of them were women.

Many women took up the exotic game Mah-Jongg instead of bridge.

Entertainment and the Arts

The Roaring Twenties are also remembered as the Jazz Age. Pioneered by African Americans, jazz music had begun to develop a few years earlier in New Orleans. Jazz spread to Chicago and across the country. It inspired new dances, such as the Charleston, and influenced movies, books, and fashion. Jazz music was popular in illegal nightclubs where people went to drink alcohol. The birth of broadcast radio in 1920 also spurred jazz's popularity. Jazz became a lifestyle associated with immoral youth.

The Birth of Talkies

"Wait a minute! Wait a minute! You ain't heard nothin' yet!" said Al Jolson in a movie called *The Jazz Singer*. Startled moviegoers in the audience on October 6, 1927, could not believe their ears. This was the first time they had ever heard a character in a film speak. Until then, all movies had been silent. The actors moved their lips and used exaggerated gestures to show what they were saying or feeling. The action on screen was frequently interrupted by printed captions. With the introduction of spoken dialogue, movies, then called talkies, achieved a new degree of realism. Acting began to more closely resemble the way people acted in real life. Silent films had been popular

The 1929 talkie **The Lady Lies** *starred Claudette Colbert and Walter Huston.*

Radio Programs

Music programs were among the most popular radio shows during the 1920s. There was something for everyone: classical, jazz, opera, and country. One long-running radio program is the *Grand Ole Opry*, which began in 1925. It is still broadcast from Nashville every Friday and Saturday night.

with American movie audiences, but talkies led to a huge increase in ticket sales at box offices.

Not everyone welcomed the new talkies. Some actors who had built successful careers in silent film had trouble making the transition to talkies. Acting in sound films required different skills. In one case, silent movie star John Gilbert's career came to an end because movie fans could not reconcile Gilbert's romantic screen image with his high-pitched voice. Silent film comedians, such as Charlie Chaplin, star of *The Gold Rush* (1925) and other comedy hits, were especially reluctant to add sound to their films. After all, the silent comedy had been a unique and popular form of art. Chaplin continued to resist the talkies, releasing his silent classic *City Lights* in 1931. But movie producers at the major Hollywood studios were aware that the future of film was the talkie. By the end of the 1920s, they had all but abandoned the silent film. Popular silent film comedians Stan Laurel and Oliver Hardy were just as popular once they began making talkies. Even Charlie Chaplin eventually began talking on screen in *Modern Times* (1936).

Walt Disney and Mickey Mouse

In 1923, Walt Disney and his brother Roy started the Disney Brothers Studio, Hollywood's first animated cartoon studio. One day while riding on a train, Walt began drawing a cute little mouse he called Mickey on his drawing pad. On November 18, 1928, Walt Disney's *Steamboat Willie*, the world's first animated cartoon with synchronized sound, opened in New York. The cartoon featured Mickey Mouse and his girlfriend, Minnie. Sound was the key element in the movie's success. Mickey's fame quickly spread far and wide. In years to come, the Walt Disney entertainment empire—movie studios, TV network, and world-famous theme parks—would be built upon the popularity of the cute little mouse.

Jazz: America's First Original Art Form

With its strong beat and rhythmic syncopation, jazz was the most popular music of the time. Jazz was African Americans' gift to the world. The earliest jazz originated in New Orleans. Its musical elements were derived from African-American brass marching bands and ragtime music from the saloons. Known as Dixieland, it was characterized by several musicians simultaneously playing their own improvisations based on the melody and chord pattern of the tune.

By the middle of the decade, flappers and other patrons of the speakeasies were enjoying the lively jazz sounds of Louis "Satchmo" Armstrong and his Hot Five. The Hot Five consisted of Louis Armstrong on cornet (a type of trumpet), Kid Ory on trombone, Johnny St. Cyr on banjo, Johnny Dodds on clarinet, and Armstrong's wife, Lil, on piano.

Although many jazz fans consider Louis Armstrong the jazz world's greatest trumpet player, he was also a great singer. He had a unique, gravelly voice. Armstrong invented the jazz style of wordless singing known as scat. In it, the singer can imitate a horn solo or make use of other sounds or nonsense syllables. Other jazz singers, such as Ella Fitzgerald, would later become famous for their scat singing. What especially endeared Louis Armstrong to millions of fans around the world was his good-humored clowning.

Other important African-American musicians of the 1920s include the great blues singer Bessie Smith and jazz pianist-composers Duke Ellington, "Jelly Roll" Morton, and Fats Waller. Waller wrote more than four hundred songs and made around five hundred recordings during his thirty-nine years of life. Among his most famous songs are "Honeysuckle Rose" and "Ain't Misbehavin.'" Toward the end of the decade, a new type of danceable jazz that would become known as swing was becoming popular. Some people believe that the term swing originated with Duke Ellington's 1931 hit "It Don't Mean a Thing If It Ain't Got That Swing."

Many white musicians were influenced by the music of African Americans. White jazz musicians, such as Benny Goodman and Bix Beiderbecke, had a wide following. Bandleaders, such as Paul Whiteman, created smoother-sounding music that spread the appeal of jazz beyond speakeasies into the concert hall. Whiteman even hired classically trained composer George Gershwin to write a piece that wove elements of jazz rhythms and the feeling of the blues into a traditional concert piece. The world premiere of Gershwin's *Rhapsody in Blue* took place on February 12, 1924, in New York's Aeolian Concert Hall. Gershwin played the piano part accompanied by Whiteman's Palais Royal Orchestra. *Rhapsody in Blue* became one of America's most popular concert pieces.

Louis Armstrong entertained generations with his iconic sound.

The Harlem Renaissance

The 1920s were a time of such great artistic achievement for African Americans that it is often referred to as the Harlem Renaissance. During this decade, New York City's Harlem neighborhood became the cultural center for African Americans. All the top jazz and blues musicians of the 1920s played in Harlem's many nightspots. Entertainers such as Josephine Baker, Florence Mills, and Bill Robinson also performed there. In addition to the famous Cotton Club, Apollo Theater, and Savoy Ballroom, there were more than one hundred other places to listen to and dance to jazz.

The literary contributions of African Americans during this period were equally significant. Among the many fine writers living and writing in Harlem at the time was poet Langston Hughes, who wrote his famous poem "The Negro Speaks of Rivers" at the age of eighteen. Hughes later took a musical approach to writing and often sang his blues poems aloud as he wrote them. Poet Countee Cullen eloquently expressed the despair of African Americans in poems such as "Any Human to Another." Claude McKay presented a realistic portrayal of black life in his novel *Home to Harlem* (1928). Other important writers included Jean Toomer, Arna Bontemps, and Zora Neale Hurston.

Americans in Paris

Gertrude Stein, an American writer living in Paris, was reportedly the first to refer to the other Americans in Paris in the 1920s as a "lost generation." Supposedly, World War I had so shattered the moral values of society that many young Americans were now struggling to find meaning. And what better place to try to find oneself than in Paris?

Art Deco

In the mid-1920s, a new artistic movement began in France. The unique style of architecture and design, known as art deco, combined dazzling beauty with everyday function. Whereas previous styles used natural curves and flowery designs, art deco favored sleek lines and modern patterns that imitated the grace and speed of machines. Designers used elegant materials, such as glass, stainless steel, and inlaid wood.

New York City became the heart of the art deco movement. New skyscrapers, such as the Chrysler Building and the Empire State Building, were built in the style.

Art deco quickly spread across the country and could be seen in the design of train stations and movie theaters. It also influenced furniture, jewelry, and even automobiles. Art deco remained a driving force in design until the end of the 1930s.

The city of Paris, with its lively café society and atmosphere of cultural excitement, attracted American writers, artists, and composers. These and many others were drawn to Paris and sought to escape a materialistic America where alcoholic drinks were illegal and life was supposed to revolve around money and business.

Young American artists who were drawn to Paris, such as Man Ray and Alexander Calder, wanted to live and work in the same city as Pablo Picasso, Marc Chagall, and Joan Miró. New styles of art, such as cubism and surrealism, were being invented there every day. The geometrically patterned design styles on display at the Paris Art Deco exposition, which opened in 1925, would be a major influence on American architecture, interior design, furniture design, and fashion for years to come.

Young American composers, such as Aaron Copland and Virgil Thomson, wanted to study and write music in the same city as Igor Stravinsky, Darius Milhaud, and Eric Satie. And young American writers and poets made their homes in Paris because it was easier to get their works published there. Two American literary masterpieces of the 1920s were written in France: Ernest Hemingway's *The Sun Also Rises* (1926) and F. Scott Fitzgerald's *The Great Gatsby* (1925).

Gertrude Stein brought together many American artists in Paris.

Lou Gehrig signed with the New York Yankees in 1923.

Sports

The 1920s saw the rise of the modern sports hero. Americans came to cherish their favorite players. Top athletes performed before enormous crowds of cheering fans, and scandals shocked the nation.

A Baseball Scandal

Baseball was still the favorite spectator sport of millions of Americans in the 1920s even though a major scandal had shocked baseball fans at the beginning of the decade. On September 28, 1920, eight members of the Chicago White Sox admitted that they had accepted $100,000 in bribes for intentionally losing the first, second, and final games of the 1919 World Series to the Cincinnati Reds. The eight men were immediately suspended, and the team began to be referred to as the Chicago Black Sox. Baseball fans, however, soon got over their shock and focused instead on the sensational ball playing of a rising star of the baseball world.

Babe Ruth

It was Babe Ruth who would revive America's national pastime. Early in his career, the baby-faced George Herman "Babe" Ruth played for the Boston Red Sox. After the 1919 season, Boston's owner sold him to New York. During his first year with the Yankees, Ruth batted .376 and hit 54 home runs, 9 triples, and 36 doubles. He scored 158 runs, batted in 137 runs, and stole 14 bases. The following year, 1921, he did even better, hitting 59 home runs, batting in 177 runs, and had a total of 204 hits—including 44 doubles and 16 triples—for a batting average of .378. In 1923, Ruth hit 41 home runs and had a batting average of .393.

That year, he was named Most Valuable Player in the American League. In addition, the Yankees began playing in their brand new stadium in the Bronx, called Yankee Stadium. Ruth, to the delight of his fans, hit a home run on opening day. Ruth's superb playing attracted huge crowds. Fans began referring to the new stadium as

The Olympics

The 1924 Olympic Games were held in Paris, France. Athletes from forty-four nations around the world participated in the games. American athletes won forty-five gold medals to lead all countries in these games.

Babe Ruth reinvigorated America's love of baseball.

the House that Ruth Built. Throughout the rest of the decade, Ruth continued to amaze his fans, and he led the American League in home runs from 1926 to 1931. Ruth hit his record 60 home runs in 1927. After hitting his sixtieth home run, on September 30, Ruth exclaimed, "That's sixty home runs, count 'em. Sixty!"

The Yankees, with the help of the Home-Run King and another great batter named Lou Gehrig, won six pennants and three World Series championships during the 1920s.

Football

Baseball was not the only sport to attract millions of fans in the 1920s. More and more Americans were drawn to football. Helping to boost the popularity of this and other sports were the nationwide radio broadcasts of sports events. Now fans around the country could share the blow-by-blow excitement of an event as it happened rather than waiting to read the scores the next day in the newspaper.

Harold "Red" Grange, known as the Galloping Ghost, helped make professional football a popular spectator sport. Grange achieved his greatest successes as a college football player at the University of Illinois from 1923 to 1925. Fans were thrilled by his running and the apparent ease with which he scored touchdowns. During his three years at Illinois, Grange played twenty varsity games during which he ran a total of 3,637 yards and scored 31 touchdowns.

By the time he signed with the Chicago Bears in 1925, Grange had already attracted a huge following of fans. Thirty-six thousand of them paid to see him play his first game against the Chicago Cardinals on Thanksgiving Day 1925. Although the game ended in a 0–0 tie, Grange, ever the crowd pleaser, had not disappointed his fans. At the close of the season, the Bears played against the New York Giants at the Polo Grounds in New York City. Seventy thousand spectators filled the stands, and countless others had to be turned away.

The NFL

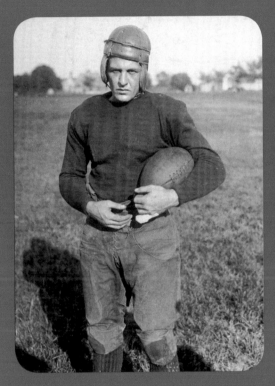

The National Football League formed in 1922. At the time, college football was far more popular. In 1925, however, the most famous college star joined the NFL when halfback Red Grange from the University of Illinois signed with the Chicago Bears. The move gave the league instant credibility and launched professional football's rise to greatness.

Boxing

The 1920s are known as the golden age of boxing. Boxing during this decade also grew into Knockouts, a popular spectator sport. Previously, boxing had been an unregulated sport associated with criminal elements and gamblers. Because boxing was banned in many places, boxing matches were often held in saloons. After World War I, laws prohibiting boxing were largely done away with, and the sport came under the control of boxing commissions. Helping to popularize boxing were two of the greatest fighters of all time, heavyweight Jack Dempsey and lightweight Benny Leonard.

Dempsey became the heavyweight champion on July 4, 1919, when he took the title away from Jess Willard. Dempsey would remain champion for the next seven years, as he knocked out one challenger after another. Dempsey was a longtime fan favorite. In addition to great boxing skills, he had a magnetic personality. His thrilling fights drew record crowds and made front-page headlines.

On September 23, 1926, Dempsey finally met his match. Dempsey and challenger Gene Tunney went a full ten rounds, and Tunney won the heavyweight title by a unanimous decision of the judges. More than 120,000 people watched; millions more listened by radio. The following year on September 22, Dempsey lost his second fight with Tunney over a controversial call.

Boxer Jack Dempsey was the heavyweight champ for much of the 1920s.

National and International Politics

World War I was supposed to have been the war to end all wars. President Woodrow Wilson had told American soldiers that they were fighting "to make the world safe for democracy." Although later events would prove these goals to have been impossible dreams, Americans in 1920 could not have known that.

The League of Nations

When Wilson proposed a League of Nations (similar to today's United Nations) to help prevent future wars, few Americans were interested. Americans had little desire to be drawn into another conflict in Europe, should one arise.

The Treaty of Versailles between the Allies and Germany was signed in 1919. Germany was forced to accept full responsibility for having started the war and had to make huge war reparations. The treaty included the provision for a League of Nations. Although Wilson campaigned around the country for the treaty's passage, the Senate failed to ratify it, as they sensed the growing isolationist sentiment among American voters. When the League of Nations met for the first time in January 1920, representatives from forty-two nations were there. There was no American representative, however, nor did

The League of Nations meets in Geneva, Switzerland, in 1920.

the United States ever join the league that Woodrow Wilson had helped create. Wilson's efforts to convince Americans of the importance of the League of Nations ruined his health. He was barely able to finish his term in office. Wilson died in 1924.

The Kellogg-Briand Pact

Late in the decade, Americans overcame their fear of foreign entanglements. They enthusiastically supported passage of the Kellogg-Briand Pact, an agreement "renouncing war as an instrument of national policy." The pact was drawn up by French Foreign Minister Aristide Briand and US Secretary of State Frank B. Kellogg. Although more than sixty nations endorsed the pact, it provided no

US Secretary of State Frank B. Kellogg co-drafted the popular but unenforcable Kellogg-Briand Pact in 1928.

measures for achieving peace beyond the moral force of world opinion. Unfortunately for the cause of world peace, the Kellogg-Briand Pact was a case of too little, too late.

The Red Scare and the Palmer Raids

A national hysteria known as the Great Red Scare swept through the United States in 1920. Many Americans, frightened by the Bolshevik Revolution in Russia, became convinced that radicals were plotting to carry out a communist revolution in America. Communism, which was based on public ownership of property such as factories and land, included a goal of world domination. This caused Americans to fear that communists would try to destroy their democratic system of government. Foreigners, especially recent immigrants, were looked on with suspicion.

An Italian immigrant named Luigi Galleani helped fuel the panic. Galleani preached the use of violence to overthrow the government. In 1919, his followers set off bombs in eight US cities, including Washington, D.C. An alarmed US government started rounding up immigrants that were deemed suspicious. Attorney General Alexander Mitchell Palmer oversaw the mass arrests, known as the Palmer Raids. Palmer himself had nearly been a victim of the bombing campaign. One of his aides was J. Edgar Hoover. Hoover would later lead the Federal Bureau of Investigation, or FBI. By early 1920, more than ten thousand immigrants had been arrested through the Palmer Raids. More than five hundred fifty, including Luigi Galleani, were deported. At the time, a jittery public approved. Today, however, many Americans believe the sweeping Palmer Raids were wrong. Many of the deported immigrants were guilty of no crime.

Sacco and Vanzetti

In 1920, Nicola Sacco and Bartolomeo Vanzetti, two Italian immigrants who openly expressed their anarchist views, were arrested for armed robbery and murder in Massachusetts. In 1921, a jury found them guilty, and the judge sentenced them to die in the electric chair. Many Americans protested the verdict, as they believed Sacco and Vanzetti had not received a fair trial. Demonstrations on their behalf took place in various cities around the country, and legal challenges led to a new hearing of the case, but the two anarchists were executed in 1927. Five decades later, in 1977, Massachusetts Governor Michael Dukakis declared publicly that Sacco and Vanzetti should not have been convicted and proclaimed a day in their honor.

New Immigration Quotas

In 1921, 1924, and 1929, the federal government passed restrictive immigration laws, supposedly to prevent potential troublemakers from entering America. But there was an obvious racist element in the new immigrant quota system. The new quota system favored immigrants from northern and western Europe, especially Anglo-Saxons. It sharply limited the number of immigrants from southern and eastern Europe, especially Jews and Italians. Asian immigrants were almost totally banned, as were immigrants from Africa. But the new immigration quotas did not apply to immigrants from the western hemisphere. Indeed, during the 1920s there was increased immigration from places such as Canada, the West Indies, and especially Mexico.

Beginning in 1924, Mexicans crossing the border into the United States had to show proof of identity and other documentation. Many Mexican immigrants complied with this requirement. But many others ignored the law, avoided the border patrol, and entered the US illegally. However, there was such a great need for cheap labor in the US, especially in the Southwest, that Mexicans were considered indispensable to the economy and were allowed to live and work there. Most Mexicans in the Southwest and California worked in agriculture or on the railroads. Others went to the Midwest and worked in steel mills, meat-packing plants, utility companies, construction, and trucking.

Ku Klux Klan

White racism in America during the 1920s reached levels not seen in many decades. Whites who hated African Americans, Jews, Catholics, and other ethnic and religious minorities joined the Ku Klux Klan, a white supremacist organization that began in the South after the Civil War. The KKK enjoyed a surge in popularity during the 1920s and spread into the Midwest. Its members burned crosses and engaged in other acts of intimidation and violence against blacks. Klansmen in the South lynched African Americans. Lynching is the execution of a person accused of a crime without first holding a trial.

Most people reject the Klan's themes of hatred and violence, and for most of its history the group has existed on the fringes of society. However, the 1920s were a restless time in America. People were still shaken by the horrors of World War I. They also feared communism and immigrants. The KKK used these fears to recruit new members.

By 1924, more than four million Americans were members of the Klan. And in 1925, forty thousand Klansmen dressed in their traditional white robes and hoods carried American flags and marched down Pennsylvania Avenue in Washington, D.C. Klansmen held positions of power in some local and state governments. The group also had an impact on national politics.

The Ku Klux Klan's revival did not last long. The group's violent nature and corrupt leaders disgusted many new members, who promptly quit the organization. By 1929, the KKK had once again withdrawn into the shadows of society.

Marcus Garvey

For most African Americans, the 1920s brought little relief from the poverty of previous decades. Those in the South lived in a strictly segregated society. Hoping to find better job opportunities, more than a million African Americans migrated from the mostly rural South to cities in the North. There, they faced discrimination in jobs, as well as in housing, although they had far greater opportunities than in the South. For a time in the early 1920s, many African Americans became followers of Marcus Garvey, a Jamaican who had founded the Universal Negro Improvement Association in 1914.

Garvey wanted to instill a sense of racial pride in African Americans and create an independent black economy. As self-appointed Provisional President of Africa, he planned to lead his followers in the creation of the Empire of Africa, a new African nation that would offer hope of a better life. But in 1923, before Garvey had managed to send a single African American back to Africa, he was convicted of mail fraud and sent to prison. Although Garvey was

Marcus Garvey promoted the back to Africa movement.

pardoned by President Calvin Coolidge after serving two years of his five-year sentence, his organization lost its influence.

Harding and the Teapot Dome Scandal

Republican presidential candidate Warren G. Harding won the 1920 election by a landslide vote. Americans were in no mood for the Democrats' plans for involving the country in the League of Nations. They felt that Woodrow Wilson, a former college professor, had betrayed them by leading the nation into World War I. They liked Harding, who seemed to be a small-town, regular guy just like the man next door.

Woodrow Wilson's Secretary of the Interior Albert Fall (far left) was convicted of accepting bribes in the Teapot Dome scandal.

Harding said he wanted nothing more than to bring the country back to normalcy. To him, this meant an isolationist country in which America would withdraw from world affairs and the federal government would help promote the growth of big business. And Harding kept his promise. Once in office, Harding repealed wartime taxes. He created a federal agency to assist veterans. He also supported tight limits on immigration to the United States. Unfortunately, he went too far out of his way to help his business friends. Harding's administration was notoriously corrupt.

It became involved in one scandal after another, which culminated in the infamous Teapot Dome scandal. In that episode, Harding's Secretary of the Interior, Albert Fall, accepted between $100,000 and $400,000 in bribes to lease government-controlled oil fields to his oil-business friends Harry F. Sinclair and Edward L. Doheney. The investigation of Teapot Dome and other corruption took a toll on Harding's health. In late July 1923, the president suddenly collapsed in a San Francisco hotel. He died four days later.

Prosperity Under Coolidge

Vice President Calvin Coolidge became president when Harding died. Coolidge was then elected President in 1924. The Republicans' campaign song, "Keep Cool and Keep Coolidge," was a hit with voters who admired the candidate's cool, calm demeanor. Coolidge, known as Silent Cal, did not have much to say, but apparently this appealed to Americans at the time. By now, prosperity had returned to the American economy. Voters wanted a president who would continue the pro-business policies of Harding, such as tax cuts and protective tariffs, but without the corruption. That is what they got.

Coolidge pretty much allowed business to take care of itself. And most Americans shared in the general prosperity. Between 1923 and 1928, corporate income increased by 28 percent, average unemployment never rose above 3.7 percent, industrial workers' wages increased by 8 percent, and the average workweek was shortened to forty-five hours. Meanwhile, inside the White House, Coolidge would often sit in his office with his feet up on the desk and fall asleep. The Coolidge Prosperity almost guaranteed the election of another Republican president. And in 1928, Americans voted for Republican Herbert Hoover, who seemed to promise even greater prosperity for the nation.

Hoover and the Great Depression

In March 1929, business was booming, unemployment was low, and the future looked bright. A confident President Hoover told Americans that before long "poverty will be banished from this nation." A former mining engineer and self-made millionaire, Hoover seemed to be the perfect president to oversee America's growing prosperity. He was a longtime friend of big business, as he had served as Secretary of Commerce in the administrations of Harding and Coolidge. In addition, Hoover had demonstrated compassion for the less fortunate by directing the Belgian Relief Commission and heading the US Food Administration during World War I. But things did not turn out the way Hoover had predicted. The stock market crashed in the fall of 1929, and the prosperity of the Roaring Twenties soon came to a screeching halt.

The booming economy of the 1920s had encouraged speculation in the stock market on a grand scale. Wealthy Americans were not the only ones to invest in the stock market. When it became clear how easy it was to make money in a rising market, many people who could not afford to gamble bought stocks anyway. Worse, they often bought stocks with borrowed money. The more money they made, the more they borrowed.

Wall Street messengers eagerly await news of the stock market.

Destitute Americans waited in long lines for free soup and bread.

It wasn't only individuals who were borrowing money they couldn't afford to pay back. After World War I, the nations of Europe needed money to repair the damage caused by the war. They borrowed heavily from American banks. Some of these countries, especially Germany, were unable to repay their loans. This placed strain on the US banking system.

By 1929, there was no more money left to borrow. It seemed nearly everyone was in debt. Many people could not afford to pay for past purchases, much less buy new items. Products sat unsold on store shelves, so companies started making less of their products. This meant that fewer workers were needed. As workers were laid off, demand for products dropped even further because people who had lost their jobs had no money to spend. As a result, companies stopped earning profits.

By the summer of 1929, some people began to lose confidence in the value of stocks. There were rumors that a crash was lurking just around the corner. Gradually, they began to sell their stocks, which culminated in a major sell-off on Thursday, October 24. On that day and the next, chaos and confusion ruled at the New York Stock Exchange. As stock prices fell, many investors had to come up with more cash or sell their stocks at a loss. Then on Tuesday, October 29, which became known as Black Tuesday, the bottom fell out of the market. Countless investors lost all their money.

After the stock market crash, people quickly rushed to withdraw their money from banks, which did not have enough cash on hand to pay everybody. Many banks closed. Businesses could not get the money they needed to keep operating, either. As businesses failed, more than fifteen million people lost their jobs. Like a disease, the depression spread around the globe. The glee of the Roaring Twenties was over. All that remained was hopelessness and despair. Recovery would take more than a decade.

Sadly, Herbert Hoover, who might have achieved great success in office had the good times continued, would go down in history as a relatively poor president.

Hitler and His Nazis

While most Americans in the 1920s tried to ignore what was happening in the rest of the world and enjoy prosperous times at home, people in other countries were not so fortunate. European nations struggled to rebuild economies ruined by World War I. Although Germany successfully established the democratic Weimar Republic, the economy suffered under the burden of war payments demanded by the Allies under the Treaty of Versailles. Unemployment was high, and inflation grew until German money was virtually worthless. Day by day, the value of the mark, Germany's currency, sank. It was cheaper to burn cash for heat than to buy firewood. A loaf of bread that cost less than a mark in 1918 cost more than 160 marks in 1922 and 200 billion marks in 1923! A wheelbarrow full of money was required to buy a single loaf of bread. Eventually, many Germans were unable to buy food.

Many Germans blamed their new democratic government for their problems. They said that their leaders never should have signed the peace treaty. Workers staged protests and strikes. Their rage was fueled by Adolf Hitler, the leader of the right-wing National Socialist German Workers (Nazi) Party. Hitler gained many devoted followers through his passionate speeches criticizing the government.

Hitler and his followers hated communists, socialists, and most of all, they hated Jews. On November 8, 1923, they stormed into a political rally at a beer hall in the city of Munich and tried to overthrow the government. The Nazis hoped that the German people, in their desperation, would support them. But the Beer Hall Putsch failed, and Hitler was thrown in jail for treason. By the time he was set free

During the 1920s, Adolf Hitler laid the groundwork for his destructive campaign to take over Germany and much of Europe.

after nine months, Hitler had written a book called *Mein Kampf* (My Struggle). In it, he set forth his plans for a powerful new Germany that he referred to as the Third Reich, or empire. He also stated that the Germans were Aryans, a master race. All other races, such as Jews and Gypsies, were inferior, even subhuman, in his eyes. Hitler's hateful message did not fall on deaf ears. The Nazi party slowly but surely grew.

Events in 1928 would prove especially bad for the future of Europe and the world. That year, Hitler's Nazi party won a dozen seats out of 491 in Germany's Reichstag (legislature). Perhaps this did not seem

Joseph Stalin ruthlessly dominated the Soviet Union.

very important at the time, but it was a major step in Hitler's climb to power and to eventual Nazi control of Germany.

Stalin and Mussolini

Meanwhile, Russia and Italy were already under the iron rule of brutal dictators. By 1920, the communists in Russia had won the civil war that followed the Bolshevik Revolution of 1917. In 1922, the country was named the Union of Soviet Socialist Republics (USSR), or Soviet Union. When Vladimir Lenin, the Father of the Revolution, died in 1924, a political power struggle began between two of his key followers, Leon Trotsky and Joseph Stalin. In 1928, Stalin, the ruthless Man of Steel, solidified his control of the communist party and began transforming the Soviet Union into a totalitarian regime in which the central government would control every aspect of people's lives. By 1929, Stalin was the undisputed leader of the Soviet Union, and Trotsky was forced into exile.

By 1928, Benito Mussolini had gained total power as *Il Duce* (the leader), or the dictator of Italy. Mussolini's rise to power began early in the decade. He and his followers, known as Blackshirts, carried out a campaign of terror against communists and socialists. In 1922, Mussolini had led fifty thousand fascists in a march on Rome, where he demanded that King Victor Emmanuel III put him in charge of the government.

Once in power, Mussolini began to get rid of Italy's democratic system. He banned labor unions and political parties that opposed his own, and he imposed strict government censorship on the media. Anyone who failed to follow fascist rules received brutal punishment. All that mattered was the glory of Italy and its all-powerful leader. Young people were taught fascist beliefs in school. He became popular with many Italians because he got things done. So while their democracy was disappearing before their eyes, many did not object. After all, working conditions improved, the economy grew stronger, and best of all, the trains ran on time.

Trouble in China

At the end of the 1920s, America and Europe were not the only places facing difficult futures. China had been in conflict throughout the decade. Those who sought to unify the country under a strong central government faced almost impossible odds. Warlords in various provinces of the huge country fought among themselves for power and influence. In an effort to gain the upper hand over the warlords, communists formed an alliance with the nationalist Kuomintang, which was led by Jiang Jieshi, or Chiang Kai-shek. The alliance did not last long.

In April 1927, Jiang's forces carried out a massacre of communists in Shanghai, and the two groups became bitter enemies. Shortly after Jiang became President of the Nationalist Republic of China in 1928, the communists and nationalists began fighting a bloody civil war that would last for many years.

Mohandas Gandhi

Trouble of a different sort was brewing in another part of Asia during the 1920s. India was a part of the British Empire at that time, but demands for independence were spreading. Leading the growing independence movement was Mohandas K. Gandhi, whom Indians referred to as the *Mahatma* (Great Soul). Gandhi preached nonviolence as the most effective way to achieve independence. He called his approach *satyagraha* ("truth force" or passive resistance). Gandhi urged Indians to engage in nonviolent civil disobedience to protest unjust British laws. He encouraged Indians to boycott British cloth and weave their own instead.

Benito Mussolini

Mussolini came from humble beginnings. He was the son of a working class couple in rural Italy. As a boy, he showed intelligence but also a quick temper. When he grew up, Mussolini tried to be a schoolteacher. That did not work out, so instead he became a newspaper editor. Mussolini found he had a special talent for swaying people with his words. With his writings, Mussolini exploited the hopes and fears of the Italian people.

He told them that Italy was in danger from communism. He also wrote that Italy could be a great empire, just as ancient Rome had once been, if only it had the right leader. Mussolini attracted followers because he made it appear as if he had the answers to all of Italy's problems.

Gandhi practiced what he preached. He refused to pay British taxes or vote in elections. He led strikes and protest demonstrations and engaged in hunger strikes. He was often jailed for his actions. Unfortunately, some Indians did not always refrain from violence, and some protests led to bloody riots. Gandhi's nonviolent struggle would continue for several decades, and the goal of an independent India would finally be achieved in the late 1940s.

Gandhi led the Indian independence movement through nonviolence.

Hirohito Ascends to the Throne

The 1920s were a difficult period in Japan. There was political turmoil, many people had no work, and a devastating earthquake destroyed the cities of Tokyo and Yokohama in 1923.

In December 1926, twenty-five-year-old prince Hirohito succeeded his father to become Japan's new emperor. As emperor, Hirohito would be the country's supreme ruler, however, since Japanese legend held that the emperor descended from the gods, ruling the country was considered too trivial a pastime. Japanese military leaders used this belief to slowly take control of the nation. Privately Hirohito complained of the military's growing power, yet he did little to stop it.

In the coming years, Japanese society would fall under the spell of the armed forces, whose goal was to expand the Japanese empire. Factories would produce nothing but war supplies. Japanese citizens were lulled into believing that foreigners were inferior. People were told to work hard and think of nothing but the glory of Japan. Emperor Hirohito seemed to support these warlike ideas. He often appeared in public wearing a military uniform. During the 1930s, Japan would invade China. Japan's leaders also sought to expand their control into the Pacific Ocean. In December 1941, Japanese forces would attack the United States at Pearl Harbor, Hawaii. These actions would cause much death and suffering. Under Hirohito's rule, Japan would know the darkest time in its long history.

Advances in Science, Technology, and Medicine

The 1920s saw many important scientific and medical advances. Chief among them were the discovery of penicillin and insulin and the successful treatment of polio. The universe expanded, thanks to discoveries in astronomy. But this decade will be forever remembered as a time when science was put on trial.

The Monkey Trial

On April 24, 1925, John T. Scopes, a high school science teacher in Dayton, Tennessee, gave a classroom lecture on Charles Darwin's theory of evolution. Darwin said that all species, including humans, evolved from common ancestors. The concept defied the Bible's description of human creation. Scopes was promptly arrested for teaching Darwin's theory. In March 1925, the state of Tennessee, catering to the wishes of Fundamentalist Christians, had passed a law forbidding the teaching of evolution in public schools. Fundamentalists, who believe in a literal interpretation of the Bible, regard Darwin's theory about human descent from a lower order of primate as heresy.

The American Civil Liberties Union (ACLU) hired famed attorney Clarence Darrow to defend Scopes. The state's prosecutors hired William Jennings Bryan, a former presidential candidate and

John Scopes was arrested for teaching Darwin's theory of evolution.

Secretary of State. During the two-week so-called Monkey Trial, which began on July 10, 1925, Darrow poked numerous holes in the case of Bryan, who presented himself as a biblical expert. Bryan's answers to Darrow's questions about the Bible often sounded ridiculous and caused laughter in the courtroom. Although Scopes was found guilty and sentenced to pay a fine of $100, Darrow had succeeded in arousing the public's interest in Darwin's theory of evolution because the trial had received so much attention in the press. More than two hundred newspaper reporters had covered the event, and radio stations had carried it nationwide. Eventually, Darwin's theory became a standard part of most school science programs. Bryan died of a heart attack five days after the trial. Tennessee's law prohibiting the teaching of evolution was not repealed until 1967.

Charles Darwin

English naturalist Charles Darwin became famous for his theory that all species of life evolved over time from common ancestors. Darwin developed his ideas about evolution after studying birds, iguanas, and other creatures on the Galápagos Islands during the 1830s.

Charles Darwin's theory of evolution is widely accepted today.

Hubble and an Expanding Universe

As recently as the 1920s, people believed that the Milky Way galaxy, in which earth, the other planets, the sun, and all the stars are located, was the entire universe and that it had always existed in a constant, relatively stable form. But in 1924, American astronomer Edwin Hubble made a startling announcement. The previous year, he had learned that the fuzzy points of light, or nebulae, he had been observing through a hundred-inch reflecting telescope at Mount Wilson in California were actually clusters of stars. And he concluded that these clusters of stars were individual galaxies. Indeed, the Milky Way was just one among many galaxies, and Hubble had figured out the distance to nine of the nearest ones.

Then Hubble made another incredible discovery. In 1929, he announced that the universe is expanding with the galaxies rushing away from each other. The farther away a galaxy is from us, the faster it is moving. This ratio is now known as the Hubble constant. Hubble's discovery later led scientists to theorize that the universe had begun in a big bang and that it has been expanding ever since. Today, we know that there are at least one hundred billion galaxies that can be seen by telescope, and each galaxy contains about one hundred billion stars. Thanks to Hubble, we can see how truly vast the universe is.

Television

In the 1920s, Americans were still excited about their amazing new radios. But work was progressing on the development of an even more amazing device. In 1923, David Sarnoff, who would become President of the Radio Corporation of America, or RCA, in 1930, made the following prediction, "I believe that television, which is the technical name for seeing as well as hearing by radio, will come to pass in the future." That year, a Russian immigrant by

Edwin Hubble discovered there are many galaxies besides our own.

King Tut's Tomb

Ancient Egyptian kings were called pharaohs. Tutankhamun was a very young pharaoh who lived in the fourteenth century BCE. The exact dates are not known, but some sources suggest he ruled from 1343 to 1333 BCE. Experts believe he died as a teenager due to complications from an injury.

In 1922, British archaeologists uncovered his hidden tomb. The discovery made Tutankhamun the best-known pharaoh. It also sparked the modern world's fascination with ancient Egypt. Archaeologist Howard Carter found the tomb buried in the Egyptian desert. Carter and his financial sponsor, Lord Carnarvon, were the first people to enter the elaborate gravesite in more than three thousand years. Once inside, they found thousands of priceless objects. They also found Tutankhamun's mummy and his now-famous gold mask.

the name of Vladimir Zworykin invented the first television camera. He called it the iconoscope and applied for a patent. In 1924, Zworykin patented the kinescope, a television picture tube using a cathode-ray tube, or CRT. The following year, he applied for a patent for the color television, which was granted in 1928.

Television was first introduced to the public in 1928, although on a very limited scale. That year, the Daven Corporation of Newark, New Jersey, offered for sale the first commercial television receiver for $75. Also that year, television station WZXAD in Schenectady, New York, offered the first scheduled television service, which broadcasted the news and the first televised play, J. Hartley Manners's *The Queen's Messenger*. Although television would not become widely available until the 1940s, Sarnoff's prediction proved to be remarkably accurate.

The Holland Tunnel

On November 13, 1927, people in New York and New Jersey were able to drive their cars under the Hudson River without getting wet! On that day, the world's first underwater automobile tunnel opened for traffic. The Holland Tunnel, named after Clifford Milburn Holland, the chief engineer of the tunnel, connected Manhattan to New Jersey. A system of fans and suction ducts were built into the tunnel's twin tubes in order to ventilate the interior of the tunnel. Ten years later, another tunnel connecting New Jersey and Manhattan under the Hudson River, the Lincoln Tunnel, opened to drivers.

Iron Lung

In 1928, Philip Drinker and Louis Agassiz Shaw created a machine that could help people breathe. At the time, many people, including soon-to-be-President Franklin D. Roosevelt, suffered from polio (poliomyelitis), a disease of the central nervous system that caused paralysis. Often, the lungs were affected, and it became difficult or impossible to breathe. Drinker and Shaw's machine, called an iron lung, helped people breathe. The first iron lung was built with an iron box and two vacuum cleaners. The patient would lie in the iron box chamber, and the vacuum pump pushed air inside, which caused the lungs to inflate. Many lives were saved by the iron lung, which prevented people from suffocating.

Penicillin and Insulin

One day in September 1928, Alexander Fleming, a Scottish bacteriologist, was about to throw away a culture plate he had prepared several weeks earlier with the common infectious bacterium known as *Staphylococcus aureus* when something caught his eye. When he took a closer look, he noticed that there were spots of mold growing near the edge of the plate, and the bacteria near the mold had been killed. For many years, Fleming had worked to discover a substance that would destroy disease-causing bacteria. Suddenly, by chance, he seemed to have found what he was searching for.

He identified the mold as *Penicillium notatum*, a mold found on Camembert cheese. He called the bacteria-fighting substance in the mold penicillin. Unfortunately, at the time, Fleming was not able to find a practical method of extracting it from the mold. It would be many years later in the 1940s that Fleming and his colleagues Howard Walker Florey and Ernst Boris Chain would find a way to purify penicillin. The discovery would eventually save millions of lives from infection.

Another important scientific discovery during this decade changed the fate of those who suffer from diabetes. Before 1922, doctors had no way to give insulin to diabetes patients, who face illness, coma, and death because of their inability to produce proper amounts. In

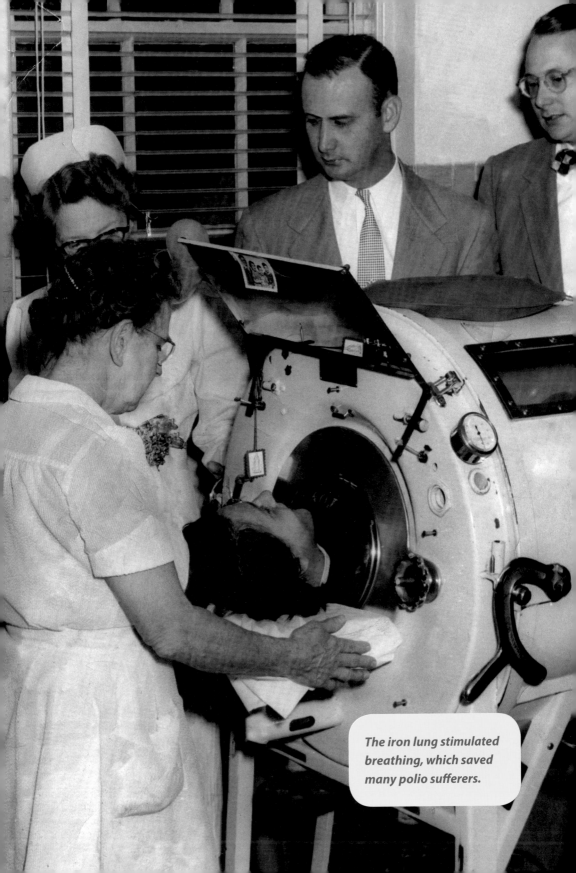

The iron lung stimulated breathing, which saved many polio sufferers.

Alexander Fleming
discovered the antibiotic
penicillin.

that year, scientists at the University of Toronto in Canada made an amazing breakthrough. They learned how to convert animal insulin for human use. With this discovery, diabetes no longer meant a slow and certain death. Instead, it became a highly treatable disease. Today, millions of diabetic people lead happy and normal lives thanks to insulin injections.

Conclusion

The decade of 1920 to 1929 is often viewed as a wild and happy time in the United States. Americans were relieved that the Great War was over. By 1920, they were ready to cast aside all memories of the war and celebrate and enjoy life. The Roaring Twenties were a glamorous and exciting time. People avidly followed the accomplishments of their favorite athletes. Charles Lindbergh was celebrated as a national hero for his solo flight across the Atlantic. Americans enjoyed attending movies and listening to radio broadcasts. Women gained new rights and a greater role in public society. Scientific advances meant a higher quality of life.

Beneath the glittering exterior, however, there were many problems. The American experiment with Prohibition led to the widespread popularity of the speakeasy, which in turn provided a setting for the exciting new sounds of jazz and a place for flappers and others to kick up their heels to the dance craze known as the Charleston. Unfortunately, the speakeasy also provided a way for gangsters to grow rich selling bootleg whiskey, and this led to the rise of organized crime and mob violence.

The 1920s was a time in which America retreated in isolation from the troubles of the world. A series of conservative Republican administrations in Washington, D.C., catered to the interests of big business, and many corporations grew powerful and prosperous. However, many Americans went deeply into debt purchasing consumer products, such as washing machines and record players. Many people tried to get rich by speculating in a rising stock market and found, to their sorrow, that nothing goes up forever. At the end of the decade, the US

The Roaring Twenties also came to be known as the Jazz Age.

stock market crashed. This was the first crisis of the Great Depression. The great stock market crash of 1929 seemed to guarantee that the next decade would not be at all like the Roaring Twenties.

In fact, the next decade, 1930 to 1939, would be a troubled time for the United States and the world. Millions of people were out of work and could barely find enough food to survive. In 1932, Franklin D. Roosevelt was elected President of the United States. Roosevelt soon created a bold plan called the New Deal, which he hoped would end the Great Depression. Roosevelt spoke often to the nation on the radio. He encouraged people and gave many Americans hope that better times were ahead.

Despite the president's efforts, the Depression would continue through the decade. In other countries, the financial crisis created political turmoil. In Germany and Japan, dangerous men used the chaos to seize power. As the 1930s ended, the world plunged into a second World War. World War II would become the deadliest conflict in human history.

Of course, the people of the 1920s did not know what was to come. Most Americans simply enjoyed their prosperity, freedom, and the fun and excitement of the times.

Timeline

1920   In January, the League of
Nations holds its first meet-
ing. On January 3, Babe Ruth
is traded to the New York
Yankees. On August 18, the
Nineteenth Amendment to
the Constitution is ratified,
which gives women the right
to vote in the United States.
On September 28, eight
members of the Chicago

White Sox admit to accepting bribes to lose in the 1919
World Series. In November, radio station KDKA broadcasts
the first scheduled radio program. Republican Warren G.
Harding wins election to the presidency on a platform urg-
ing a return to normalcy. The Red Scare begins. Sacco and
Vanzetti are arrested.

1921   Margaret Sanger founds the
American Birth Control
League.

1922   British archaeologist Howard
Carter discovers King Tut's
tomb in Egypt. Russia is
renamed the Union of Soviet

Socialist Republics, or Soviet Union. Benito Mussolini leads a march on Rome and demands that he be put in charge of the government.

1923 More than five hundred public radio stations are broadcasting. Archaeologist Howard Carter visits the United States on a lecture tour, which sets off a King Tut fad. Babe Ruth is named the Most Valuable Player in the American League.

Yankee Stadium opens in the Bronx, New York. Marcus Garvey, leader of the back to Africa separatist movement, is convicted of mail fraud and sent to prison. In August, President Harding dies in office. Vice President Calvin Coolidge becomes president. In November, the Nazi party tries unsuccessfully to overthrow the German government. Vladimir Zworykin invents the first television camera, called the iconoscope.

1924 In February, George Gershwin's *Rhapsody in Blue* premieres in New York City. At the height of the Charleston craze, a Charleston marathon at New York's Roseland ballroom lasts for twenty-four hours. Richard Leo Simon and Max Lincoln Schuster publish *The Crossword Puzzle Book*, which starts a crossword puzzle craze. Psychotherapist Emile Coué's book *Self-Mastery Through Conscious Auto-Suggestion* wins many followers. Alvin Kelly starts the flagpole-sitting craze. Woodrow Wilson dies. In November, Coolidge is elected president. Vladimir Lenin, leader of the Soviet Union, dies. Edwin Hubble announces that the Milky Way is just one of many galaxies. Vladimir Zworykin invents the kinescope. The Olympic Games are held in Paris.

1925   Charlie Chaplin's *The Gold Rush* is released. F. Scott Fitzgerald's *The Great Gatsby* is published. Harold "Red" Grange signs with the Chicago Bears, which attracts a huge following and helps make professional football a popular spectator sport in the United States. The *Grand Ole Opry* begins radio broadcasts every Friday and Saturday. Forty thousand members of the Ku Klux Klan march in a parade through Washington, D.C. For two weeks, starting

on July 25, the Scopes Monkey Trial takes place. The first Art Deco design appears at a Paris arts show.

1926   Ernest Hemingway's *The Sun Also Rises* is published. On September 23, heavyweight boxing champion Jack Dempsey loses to Gene Tunney.

1927   Ford introduces the Model A, an improvement on the Model T. In April, Jiang Jieshi's nationalist forces attack communist forces at Shanghai, which permanently separates the two groups. On May 20, Charles Lindbergh makes the first solo non-stop transatlantic flight from New York to Paris, France. On September 30, Babe Ruth hits his then-record sixtieth home run for the season. On October 6, the first spoken-word film, *The Jazz Singer*, opens in theaters. Sacco and Vanzetti are executed.

1928   Claude McKay publishes *Home to Harlem*. In August, several nations sign the Kellogg-Briand Pact, which attempts to outlaw war as a means of solving international problems. In September, Alexander Fleming accidentally happens upon the mold that will eventually lead to the development of antibiotics. In November, Republican Herbert Hoover wins the election to the presidency. Nazi party candidates win a dozen seats in the German legislature. Joseph Stalin takes control of the Soviet Communist party. Jiang Jieshi becomes President of the Nationalist Republic of China. The Chinese Civil War begins.

Vladimir Zworykin receives a patent for his color television. The Daven Corporation offers the first commercial television for sale.

1929   Joseph Stalin becomes the dictator of the Soviet Union. There are more than 23 million cars in America. Edwin Hubble announces that the universe is expanding. On February 14, the St. Valentine's Massacre, ordered by Al Capone, takes place in Chicago. In March, President Hoover predicts a coming end to poverty. During the summer, some people begin to sell their stocks. On

October 24, a large sell-off of stocks occurs. On October 29, the stock market crashes, setting off the Great Depression.

Glossary

art deco—Architectural and design style begun in the 1920s that favors sleek lines and modern patterns using materials such as glass, stainless steel, and inlaid wood.

dictator—A ruler with absolute over his or her country, often obtaining this power with force.

evolution—Theory proposed by Charles Darwin that says all species evolved from common ancestors.

fascism—A radical form of authoritarian nationalism characterized by devotion to a strong leader, ultra-nationalism, and the use of an aggressive military to defend national interests.

flapper—Young women of the 1920s who defied conventional behavior and dress by showing their ankles, cutting their hair, and dancing to jazz.

gangster—A member of an organized band of violent criminals.

heresy—Belief that contradicts an accepted religious theory.

insulin—A hormone produced by the body that regulates blood glucose.

iron lung—Medical device used particularly to provide artificial respiration for polio patients.

Ku Klux Klan—A white supremacist organization that began in the South after the Civil War whose members intimidated and terrorized African Americans, Catholics, immigrants, and Jews.

mob—Slang term for a group of gangsters or organized criminals.

Nazi—A member of Adolf Hitler's political party.

penicillin—A group of antibiotics used to treat bacterial infections and other serious diseases.

Prohibition—An era characterized by the prevention of the manufacture and sale of alcohol.

ratify—To accept and sign into law.

scat—Improvisational vocals in jazz music.

speakeasy—A nightclub that illegally and secretly sold alcohol during the Prohibition era.

suffrage—The right to vote in elections.

talkie—A motion picture with a soundtrack.

Further Reading

Books

Allen, Frederick Lewis. *Only Yesterday: An Informal History of the 1920s.* New York: Harper Perennial Modern Classics, 2010.

Caravantes, Peggy. *The Many Faces of Josephine Baker.* Chicago.: Chicago Review Press, 2015.

Mackrell, Judith. *Flappers: Six Women of a Dangerous Generation.* New York: Farrar, Straus and Giroux, 2015.

Rowell, Rebecca. *Charles Lindberg.* Edina, Minn.: ABDO Publishing, 2010.

Sherman, Ed. *Babe Ruth's Called Shot.* Guilford, Conn.: Globe Pequot Press, 2014.

Yancey, Diane. *Art Deco.* Detroit, Mich.: Lucent Books, 2011.

Web Sites

whitehouse.gov/history/presidents/cc30.html
Official fact sheet about Calvin Coolidge's presidency.

lcweb2.loc.gov/ammem/coolhtml/coolhome.html
Library of Congress page about the 1920s.

pbs.org/wgbh/amex/monkeytrial/
Companion site to PBS's American Experience film examining the Scopes Monkey Trial.

Movies

The Great Gatsby, Directed by Baz Luhrmann. Burbank, Calif.: Warner
    Brothers Pictures, 2013.

    Movie adaptation of F. Scott Fitzgerald's Jazz Age novel.

Inherit the Wind. Directed by Stanley Kramer. Beverly Hills, Calif.:
    United Artists, 1960.

    Dramatic depiction of the Scopes Monkey Trial.

Index

flappers, 8, 19, 20, 22, 23, 33, 82
Fleming, Alexander, 78
Ford, Henry, 12

G

Gandhi, Mohandas K., 66
gangsters, 7, 16, 18, 82
Garvey, Marcus, 54
Gehrig, Lou, 44
Germany, 8, 48, 61, 62, 63, 65, 84
Gershwin, George, 34
Gilbert, John, 32
Grange, Harold "Red", 44, 45
Great Depression, 58, 84
Great Gatsby, The, 38

H

Harding, Warren G., 7, 56, 57, 58
Hardy, Oliver, 32
Harlem Renaissance, 7, 8, 36
Hemingway, Ernest, 38
Hitler, Adolf, 62, 63, 65
Holland Tunnel, 77
Hoover, Herbert, 58, 62
Hubble, Edwin, 74
Hughes, Langston, 36
Hurston, Zora Neale, 36

I

immigration laws, 8, 52, 53, 57
iron lung, 77, 78

J

jazz, 7, 16, 30, 32, 33, 34, 36, 82
Jazz Singer, The, 30

Jiang Jieshi, 66
Jolson, Al, 30

K

King Tutankhamen, 76
Ku Klux Klan, 8, 53, 54

L

Laurel, Stan, 32
League of Nations, 48, 56
League of Women Voters, 19
Lenin, Vladimir, 65
Leonard, Benny, 45
Lindbergh, Charles, 12, 13, 28, 82

M

Mah-Jongg, 27
McKay, Claude, 36
Mills, Florence, 36
Miró, Joan, 38
Model T Ford, 12
Moran, Bugs, 16
Morton, "Jelly Roll," 34
Mussolini, Benito, 65, 67

N

Nazis,62, 63, 65
New York Stock Exchange, 61
New York Yankees, 42, 44
Nineteenth Amendment, 19

P

penicillin, 70, 78
Picasso, Pablo, 38